Francis Frith's

Leicestershire & Rutland
LIVING MEMORIES

photographs of the mid-twentieth century

Francis Frith's
Leicestershire & Rutland
LIVING MEMORIES

Ken Wheatley

First published in the United Kingdom in 2002 by
Frith Book Company Ltd

Hardback Edition 2002
ISBN 1-85937-500-6

British Library Cataloguing in Publication Data

Francis Frith's Leicestershire & Rutland Living Memories
Ken Wheatley

Frith Book Company Ltd
Frith's Barn, Teffont,
Salisbury, Wiltshire SP3 5QP
Tel: +44 (0) 1722 716 376
Email: info@francisfrith.co.uk
www.francisfrith.co.uk

Printed and bound in Great Britain

Front Cover: Leicester, The Clock Tower and Belgrave Gate c1950 L144006

contents

Francis Frith: Victorian Pioneer

FRANCIS FRITH, Victorian founder of the world-famous photographic archive, was a complex and multi-talented man. A devout Quaker and a highly successful Victorian businessman, he was both philosophic by nature and pioneering in outlook.

By 1855 Francis Frith had already established a wholesale grocery business in Liverpool, and sold it for the astonishing sum of £200,000, which is the equivalent today of over £15,000,000. Now a multi-millionaire, he was able to indulge his passion for travel. As a child he had pored over travel books written by early explorers, and his fancy and imagination had been stirred by family holidays to the sublime mountain regions of Wales and Scotland. 'What a land of spirit-stirring and enriching scenes and places!' he had written. He was to return to these scenes of grandeur in later years to 'recapture the thousands of vivid and tender memories', but with a different purpose. Now in his thirties, and captivated by the new science of photography, Frith set out on a series of pioneering journeys to the Nile regions that occupied him from 1856 until 1860.

Intrigue and Adventure

He took with him on his travels a specially-designed wicker carriage that acted as both dark-room and sleeping chamber. These far-flung journeys were packed with intrigue and adventure. In his life story, written when he was sixty-three, Frith tells of being held captive by bandits, and of fighting 'an awful midnight battle to the very point of surrender with a deadly pack of hungry, wild dogs'. Sporting flowing Arab costume, Frith arrived at Akaba by camel seventy years before Lawrence, where he encountered 'desert princes and rival sheikhs, blazing with jewel-hilted swords'.

During these extraordinary adventures he was assiduously exploring the desert regions bordering the Nile and patiently recording the antiquities and peoples with his camera. He was the first photographer to venture beyond the sixth cataract. Africa was still the mysterious 'Dark Continent', and Stanley and Livingstone's historic meeting was a decade into the future. The conditions for picture taking confound belief. He laboured for hours in his wicker dark-room in the sweltering heat of the desert, while the volatile chemicals fizzed dangerously in their trays. Often he was forced to work in remote tombs and caves where conditions were cooler. Back in London he exhibited his photographs and was 'rapturously cheered' by members of the Royal Society. His reputation as a photographer was made overnight. An eminent modern historian has likened their impact on the population of the time to that on our own generation of the first photographs taken on the surface of the moon.

Venture of a Life-Time

Characteristically, Frith quickly spotted the opportunity to create a new business as a specialist publisher of photographs. He lived in an era of immense and sometimes violent change. For the poor in the early part of Victoria's reign work was a drudge and the hours long, and people had precious little free time to enjoy themselves. Most had no transport other than a cart or gig at their disposal, and had not travelled far beyond the boundaries of their own town or village. However,

by the 1870s, the railways had threaded their way across the country, and Bank Holidays and half-day Saturdays had been made obligatory by Act of Parliament. All of a sudden the ordinary working man and his family were able to enjoy days out and see a little more of the world.

With characteristic business acumen, Francis Frith foresaw that these new tourists would enjoy having souvenirs to commemorate their days out. In 1860 he married Mary Ann Rosling and set out with the intention of photographing every city, town and village in Britain. For the next thirty years he travelled the country by train and by pony and trap, producing fine photographs of seaside resorts and beauty spots that were keenly bought by millions of Victorians. These prints were painstakingly pasted into family albums and pored over during the dark nights of winter, rekindling precious memories of summer excursions.

The Rise of Frith & Co

Frith's studio was soon supplying retail shops all over the country. To meet the demand he gathered about him a small team of photographers, and published the work of independent artist-photographers of the calibre of Roger Fenton and Francis Bedford. In order to gain some understanding of the scale of Frith's business one only has to look at the catalogue issued by Frith & Co in 1886: it runs to some 670 pages, listing not only many thousands of views of the British Isles but also many photographs of most European countries, and China, Japan, the USA and Canada – note the sample page shown above from the hand-written *Frith & Co* ledgers detailing pictures taken. By 1890 Frith had created the greatest specialist photographic publishing company in the

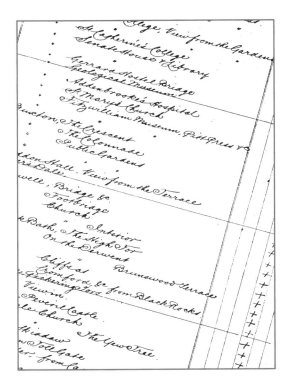

world, with over 2,000 outlets – more than the combined number that Boots and W H Smith have today! The picture on the right shows the *Frith & Co* display board at Ingleton in the Yorkshire Dales. Beautifully constructed with mahogany frame and gilt inserts, it could display up to a dozen local scenes.

Postcard Bonanza

The ever-popular holiday postcard we know today took many years to develop. In 1870 the Post Office issued the first plain cards, with a pre-printed stamp on one face. In 1894 they allowed other publishers' cards to be sent through the mail with an attached adhesive halfpenny stamp. Demand grew rapidly, and in 1895 a new size of postcard was permitted called the court card, but there was little room for illustration. In 1899, a

year after Frith's death, a new card measuring 5.5 x 3.5 inches became the standard format, but it was not until 1902 that the divided back came into being, with address and message on one face and a full-size illustration on the other. *Frith & Co* were in the vanguard of postcard development, and Frith's sons Eustace and Cyril continued their father's monumental task, expanding the number of views offered to the public and recording more and more places in Britain, as the coasts and countryside were opened up to mass travel.

Francis Frith died in 1898 at his villa in Cannes, his great project still growing. The archive he created continued in business for another seventy years. By 1970 it contained over a third of a million pictures of 7,000 cities, towns and villages. The massive photographic record Frith has left to us stands as a living monument to a special and very remarkable man.

Frith's Archive: A Unique Legacy

FRANCIS FRITH'S legacy to us today is of immense significance and value, for the magnificent archive of evocative photographs he created provides a unique record of change in 7,000 cities, towns and villages throughout Britain over a century and more. Frith and his fellow studio photographers revisited locations many times down the years to update their views, compiling for us an enthralling and colourful pageant of British life and character.

We tend to think of Frith's sepia views of Britain as nostalgic, for most of us use them to conjure up memories of places in our own lives with which we have family associations. It often makes us forget that to Francis Frith they were records of daily life as it was actually being lived in the cities, towns and villages of his day. The Victorian age was one of great and often bewildering change for ordinary people, and though the pictures evoke an impression of slower times, life was as busy and hectic as it is today.

We are fortunate that Frith was a photographer of the people, dedicated to recording the minutiae of everyday life. For it is this sheer wealth of visual data, the painstaking chronicle of changes in dress, transport, street layouts, buildings, housing, engineering and landscape that captivates us so much today. His remarkable images offer us a powerful link with the past and with the lives of our ancestors.

Today's Technology

Computers have now made it possible for Frith's many thousands of images to be accessed almost instantly. In the Frith archive today, each photograph is carefully 'digitised' then stored on a CD Rom. Frith archivists can locate a single photograph amongst thousands within seconds. Views can be catalogued and sorted under a variety of categories of place and content to the immediate benefit of researchers.

Inexpensive reference prints can be created for them at the touch of a mouse button, and a wide range of books and other printed materials assembled and published for a wider, more general readership - in the next twelve months over a hundred Frith local history titles will be published! The day-to-day workings of the archive are very different from how they were in Francis Frith's time: imagine the herculean task of sorting through eleven tons of glass negatives as Frith had to do to locate a particular sequence of pictures!

See Frith at www.francisfrith.co.uk

Yet the archive still prides itself on maintaining the same high standards of excellence laid down by Francis Frith, including the painstaking cataloguing and indexing of every view.

It is curious to reflect on how the internet now allows researchers in America and elsewhere greater instant access to the archive than Frith himself ever enjoyed. Many thousands of individual views can be called up on screen within seconds on one of the Frith internet sites, enabling people living continents away to revisit the streets of their ancestral home town, or view places in Britain where they have enjoyed holidays. Many overseas researchers welcome the chance to view special theme selections, such as transport, sports, costume and ancient monuments.

We are certain that Francis Frith would have heartily approved of these modern developments in imaging techniques, for he himself was always working at the very limits of Victorian photographic technology.

The Value of the Archive Today

Because of the benefits brought by the computer, Frith's images are increasingly studied by social historians, by researchers into genealogy and ancestory, by architects, town planners, and by teachers and schoolchildren involved in local history projects.

In addition, the archive offers every one of us an opportunity to examine the places where we and our families have lived and worked down the years. Highly successful in Frith's own era, the archive is now, a century and more on, entering a new phase of popularity.

The Past in Tune with the Future

Historians consider the Francis Frith Collection to be of prime national importance. It is the only archive of its kind remaining in private ownership and has been valued at a million pounds. However, this figure is now rapidly increasing as digital technology enables more and more people around the world to enjoy its benefits.

Francis Frith's archive is now housed in an historic timber barn in the beautiful village of Teffont in Wiltshire. Its founder would not recognize the archive office as it is today. In place of the many thousands of dusty boxes containing glass plate negatives and an all-pervading odour of photographic chemicals, there are now ranks of computer screens. He would be amazed to watch his images travelling round the world at unimaginable speeds through network and internet lines.

The archive's future is both bright and exciting. Francis Frith, with his unshakeable belief in making photographs available to the greatest number of people, would undoubtedly approve of what is being done today with his lifetime's work. His photographs, depicting our shared past, are now bringing pleasure and enlightenment to millions around the world a century and more after his death.

Leicestershire & Rutland
An Introduction

THE local tourist bureau advertisement says that Leicester and Leicestershire are full of surprises. This, to anyone who has travelled around the picturesque towns and villages, is plainly true. Many people have described the city as having too much red brick; this may be so, but the villages within the county offer a very different picture.

Despite the many attractions on offer, Leicestershire is not a noted tourist county. Many visitors head straight for Stratford-upon-Avon, the Derbyshire Peaks or the Yorkshire Dales. Missing out on treasures like the churches at Breedon-on-the-Hill, Staunton Harold and Tickencote can only be described as unfortunate. True, there are no high, rugged hills or moors in Leicestershire, but Bradgate Park and Charnwood Forest have been described on many a postcard as 'Little Switzerland'. The rocks that make up this area are pre-Cambrian,

and it was here that a boy found the world's oldest fossil in 1957.

Leicestershire is still a panorama of bewitching beauty today. It is not hard to find traces of the county's pre- and post-conquest history in the names of settlements such as Cold Overton, Croxton Kerrial, Fenny Drayton, Husbands Bosworth, Isley Walton, Osgathorpe, Potters Marston and Wymeswold. There remain unspoilt beauty spots and haunts of delight, broad woods and hidden copses, glades where deer stand silently and nature retains her undisputed sway. These enticing nooks and shadowy woodlands are still easy to find.

Geographically, the city of Leicester can be compared to the hub of a wheel; its spokes are the roads and railways that link with the towns around it. Towns like Melton Mowbray, Market Harborough, Loughborough, Ashby and Lutterworth have strong agricultural roots, whilst

Hinckley and Coalville have an air of industry and commerce.

The Soar Valley slices the county into two more or less equal halves, and makes Leicester the place where many old roads and tracks meet. This hub has been very important, not only as a settlement but also in the history of Britain. Within twenty-five miles of the centre of the city, battles have been fought that have shaped history. Firstly, the Wars of the Roses came to an end at Bosworth, and just over the county border, the battle of Naseby concluded the Civil War. The first steam railway in the Midlands made its debut in Leicester, rubber tyres were first made here, and the jet-age was born just outside Lutterworth.

There have been many archaeological discoveries in the city and the county. In Leicester it is possible to see what is probably the largest piece of Roman masonry between Hadrian's Wall and Bath. The city's broad-spectrum of museums give us a clear picture of

the different stages in the history of English towns from the earliest times to the present day. The city was the scene of many magnificent festivals organised by the numerous religious guilds which were formed in Leicester long ago.

From the highest points in the county, Bardon Hill and Beacon Hill, we can see its main features. Here in the ancient forest of Charley, or Charnwood, there are many woods and copses of oak, beech and fir, some of which are of ancient origin. Eastwards, the ground slopes gently towards the Soar and rises again in a patchwork of fields to a plateau of wolds and rounded hills. Beyond this lies Rutland, which will be considered later.

To the west and north-west is the old coalfield area with the towns of Coalville, Ibstock and Measham, along with a host of villages which at one time depended on the local mines. Much of the western side of the county is included in the new National Forest, a long-term project that will see thousands of

Foxton, The Grand Union Canal c1960 F159003

acres returned to woodland.

If we look south and south-east, we see that the land falls away more gradually to the horizon in a broad plain broken with ridges of low hills. There is an isolated outcrop at Croft, between Leicester and Hinckley - it has been described as 'the pimple at the base of the backbone of England'. Here is one of Leicestershire's other important industries, quarrying. There is granite to be found in the county, along with sand, gravel and gypsum, which means that train-loads of stone leave the county every day.

High Leicestershire in the east is divided into two portions by the lovely little River Wreake and its tributary, the River Eye. These join the Soar near Rothley after meandering through unbroken countryside and pleasant unspoilt villages.

Agriculture is still important here, as it is elsewhere in the county: farms large and small have fine water meadows and grazing land. Dairy farming gives us the well-loved Red Leicester cheese and the king of English cheeses, Stilton. Cereal crops are also important. A crop from former times is recalled in the quaint name of the village Barton-in-the-Beans. An old proverb says: 'Shake a Leicestershire yeoman, and you will hear the beans rattle' - beans used to be the staple diet of the agricultural labourer.

The countryside is also the home of the county's emblem, the fox. It is an apt badge, for the Quorn, Atherstone, Fernie, Cottesmore and Belvoir hunts have their territories in Leicestershire and around its boundaries. Leicestershire's hunting associations have a literature of their own.

Leicester itself is one of the most ancient towns of Britain and one of the most interesting. Originally a Roman town, it had hardly grown any bigger in size by 1700 than it was in 1400. It awoke in the 1750s to have stagecoaches, newspapers, an organized cattle trade and an improved water supply. The town has always been associated with the woollen industry; the world's first worsted spinning mill was built on its river banks. This was followed soon after by the extensive hosiery, boot and shoe, and light engineering industries. Thus instead of being dependent on just one industry, the town had three. These industries let the town grow to become a city; had it not been for them, then Leicester would have been much smaller, more

Cottesmore, The Village c1965 C434382

the size of Worcester or Hereford.

Loughborough, a thriving university town, has a surprise that is almost unique. One of Britain's only two bell foundries is hidden away in a street off the centre. November 1881 saw the heaviest bell in Britain cast here. This was the hour bell for St Paul's Cathedral and is named Great Paul. At over sixteen tons, it was too heavy to travel safely by rail, so it went by horsepower to London. Loughborough also boasts a preserved main-line steam railway, and every November a traditional street fair takes over the town centre for three days.

Further along the Soar valley we come to Dishley Grange, the home of the revolutionary agriculturist Robert Bakewell; his breeding of Leicestershire sheep and cattle made them sought-after as stock for farmers in this country and abroad.

Ashby-de-la-Zouch (the French part of the name comes from the first Norman lord of the manor) has had its castle immortalised as the scene of the tournament in Scott's 'Ivanhoe'. Visited by James I, the castle also held Mary, Queen of Scots as a prisoner for some time. Not too far from here is the Abbey of Mount St Bernard, the first religious community to be established after the dissolution of the monasteries. It is the only Cistercian monastery in England.

Rutland's motto means 'much in little', which is very apt. This unspoilt gem of English countryside has been associated with its larger neighbour for many years; for twenty or so of them Rutland was combined with Leicestershire, to the consternation of many locals - even to the point where a Rutland passport was issued to maintain its independent air!

Rutland offers the interested visitor a wealth of countryside and unspoilt villages, including Rutland Water. This is the largest man-made lake in lowland England, and it is surrounded with a choice of country paths for walkers that would rival those in any other county. It was here in 2001 that the first wild osprey was hatched in England for one hunderd and fifty years; this success was due to a five-year programme to establish a breeding colony of the birds. Rutland Water, with its rich selection of bird-life, hosts the annual British Birdwatching Fair every August. With hides surrounding the lake, along with butterfly and aquatic centres, the emphasis on natural history and conservation is very strong. Trout and pike fishing are also well established.

Oakham is Rutland's county town. A visit to the great hall of its castle (built around 1190), the most complete of its kind in England and the only part of the castle to survive, is indeed surprising. Its tradition of receiving horseshoes from members of the Royal Family and peers of the realm is still observed. The earliest is said to have been given by Elizabeth I. Stocks, a butter cross and the town pump all stand in the market place in front of Oakham's well-known public school. This, like Rutland's other public school at Uppingham, was founded in 1584 by Robert Johnson, Archdeacon of Leicester.

Villages where one can enjoy unspoilt and almost timeless scenes abound in Rutland. They include Wing, with its ancient turf maze, one of only a handful in Britain; Stoke Dry, with its connections to the Gunpowder Plot; and nearby Eyebrook Reservoir, famed for being the site of dummy runs for the 'dambusters' raids during the last war. All these add up to two counties well worth visiting.

◄ **Anstey, The Nook c1965** A312009
This view shows the bank before its additional floor and new façade were added. Today's traffic has brought lights around a much-reduced traffic island, which has lost the trees and shrubs. Shops and services have been developed for the growing community that is now well-established as one of Leicester's commuter villages.

◄ **Anstey, The Pack Horse Bridge c1965** A312002
Straddling Rothley Brook, the medieval bridge is a feature of this large village that has grown considerably since the last war. Folklore tells of the machine-wrecking by a local, Ned Ludd, in the early 19th century; he was imitated by others in the area as a protest against the mechanisation of the knitting industry - hence the term 'Luddite'.

◄ **Asfordby, The Street c1955** A211010
For nearly a hundred years, the Holwell ironworks were an important focus for the village. Its self-contained agricultural origins have almost totally disappeared, and today modern housing is fairly extensive. Views such as this, however, are still easily recognisable.

Ashby-de-la-Zouch, Market Street c1965
A212020
Prominent on this main road was Rushton's poultry shop on the left. At Christmas especially, rows of pheasants, rabbits and hares hung here, along with other game, poultry and fish. Its wide choice of eggs, cheeses and seasonal accompaniments ensured a brisk trade. Sad to say, after over 140 years, Rushton's has now ceased trading. Likewise, with other shops in this view, businesses have changed.

◄ **Barrow-upon-Soar, The Bridge and the River c1960** B514033
Barrow-upon-Soar lies next to Charnwood Forest amongst fine water meadows. The village's assets attract visitors and shoppers, whilst the River Soar brings in canal cruisers. Of its sizeable population, many commute to surrounding East Midland towns.

◄ Ashby-de-la-Zouch, Bath Street c1955
A212011
19th-century Ashby was noted for its healing bromide waters; Ivanhoe Bath House was built in 1822. Close by is the monument by Sir Gilbert Scott to Lady Edith Hastings, Countess of Loudoun erected in 1879 by Ashby residents. Note the cart of linoleum ready for delivery, and the brand-new street lighting.

Belvoir Castle c1965
▼ B63004
Belvoir is home to the Manners family, Dukes of Rutland. The castle holds a lofty hilltop position surveying five counties. It is visited by many every year, and holds various special attraction days.

◄ Bitteswell, The Village c1955 B584016
This view, almost unchanged today, shows the 14th-century St Mary's Church overlooking the village greens. James Powell, the vicar from 1789 to 1844, married Mary Twining of the tea family; the lychgate, visible behind the telephone post, was built in his memory.

▼ **Bitteswell, The Man-at-Arms c1960** B584014
Houses from different eras mix well around the greens. Adjoining the village today, a huge distribution centre is developing on the former air crew training base.

▼ **Bottesford, Church Street c1960** B515240
Bottesford is tucked away in the far north-eastern corner of Leicestershire, in the middle of the magnificent Vale of Belvoir. The spire of St Mary's Church is the tallest in Leicestershire. Inside the church are the remains of generations of the Manners family, Dukes of Rutland.

▲ **Broughton Astley, Main Road c1960** B517015
Willow Cottage is still trading, although the proprietor is no longer P A Jones. The small school (note the bell in the bell-cote) has been replaced with three other larger establishments, which gives us some idea of the growth the village has experienced. Already two adjacent hamlets, Sutton-in-the-Elms and Primethorpe, have been enveloped.

◀ **Burbage, The Village c1960** B858004
Extensive development and infilling has transformed the village into more of a suburb of Hinckley today. The Infantryman memorial is still central to this view of the Anchor Inn and Bailey's the butcher's; note the little child passing the unmarked post office.

Caldecott, The Green c1955 C468002
Caldecott is situated in the rural Welland Valley; its origins go back to Roman times. The Plough Inn and the surrounding houses are mostly built of local stone and tiled with Collyweston slate.

Coalville, Leicester Road c1965 C432053
Coalville developed as a town from a railway station named Long Lane on the old Leicester-Swannington line (1832). The nearby coalmines were amongst the richest in the former Leicestershire coalfield. This view shows that there was still a wide variety of shops and trades in the 1960s whose origins lay in mid-Victorian times; today, modern retail development has replaced them.

Coalville
Belvoir Road c1965 C432042
This view shows the heart of what was the busy shopping centre of this mining
town. There was also a large brick and tile making industry in the town. In 1922
the town achieved notoriety with the 'Coalville Lion' ghost. A colossal hoax

◀ **Cosby, The Barn c1965**
C433012
This view looks towards the brook from behind the chestnut tree we can see to the left in No C433010. The ancient barn on the right bears the date 1766, but this is the date of its rebuilding; its original construction date was much earlier.

Cosby, The Brook c1965 C433010

Cosby brook runs through the centre of this pleasant village, which is a doorstep to the city; the village was the first in the county to have a conservation area. A post office, a shop and a hairdresser's still serve a larger and more varied community.

Cossington, The Village c1965 C470002

The blossom is out in this attractive village where ancient and modern homes combine harmoniously. Many visits were made here by Earl Kitchener to his parents. His father's grave lies in the churchyard. The loss of the earl on HMS 'Hampshire' in 1916 on his way to put the Russian military in order was regarded as a national calamity.

Cottesmore The Village c1955 C434009

A tractor, without a cab for the driver, hauls its trailer through the centre of the village. The houses are mostly thatched and built of stone. Bus timetables, an important part of any village, are on show next to the other essential, the village shop.

▼ **Countesthorpe, Main Street c1965** C471013
Dating from 1220, St Andrew's Church has a commanding view over the village centre. In the foreground, the pseudo-Tudor Bull's Head has Briggs' bike shop, newsagent and general store as its neighbour. Even when this photograph was taken, freshly baked bread and locally delivered milk were the order of the day.

▼ **Countesthorpe, Station Road c1965** C471024
This solidly-built Edwardian shop is still trading as the Post Office, despite some alteration; it stands on the way down to the former station site. As with many Victorian villages, the station here was a fair distance from the place it purported to serve. Much obscured by the delivery lorry is the Railway Hotel.

▲ **Earl Shilton, The Hollow c1965** E161003
The driver of the 658 Leicester to Coventry Midland Red bus service breaks his journey to await passengers in this familiar view of the centre. The 'Earl' part of the placename was added when the lands were in the possession of the Earl of Leicester during the 12th century. The recently restored memorial on the right is now more prominent.

◀ **Earl Shilton, Wood Street c1965** E161305
Adjoining the Hollow, the main A47 becomes Wood Street. Today the scene is a lot more commercial. The four Belisha beacons have been replaced by their pelican equivalent.

Empingham, Church Street c1955 E134004
Between the wars, the five hundred inhabitants of this picturesque village included a wheelwright, saddler, blacksmith and farrier, carpenter, carrier, coalman, thatcher, thresher, shepherd, milkman, baker, butcher, general storekeeper and postmaster; in 1990 only the store, post office and milkman remained. This is an indication, if it were needed, of the metamorphosis of this and of many villages in the closing years of the last century. Unchanging, though, is St Botolph's Church near the River Gwash as it watches over the limestone cottages.

◄ **Fleckney, High Street c1960** F134013
New housing estates have transformed Fleckney to the sizeable community it is today. Building now stretches far beyond the trees. Originally it had one of the first framework knitting communities of the 19th century, and the local firm, Wolsey Knitwear, had its beginnings in the village.

Empingham, Post Office Corner
c1955 E134013
Time stands still in this peaceful view of the village; but on 12 March 1470, the Battle of Loscote Field, one of many during the Wars of the Roses, was fought in the parish. There are reports of ten thousand being killed, and part of the local woods are still known as the Bloody Oaks.

Fleckney, Kilby Road
c1960 F134011
The cyclist passes the neat Victorian terraces and villas that today have all mains services. The road has been upgraded, and modern housing has appeared wherever space permits. Note the 'up to date' fencing on the right.

Foxton, The Grand Union Canal c1960 F159006
The lock-keepers' cottages served the flight on the section known as the Leicester Line. Top Lock cottage in particular has magnificent views of the rolling countryside. Cruising has become a significant leisure activity, and the shop on the left serves a busy passing trade, especially during the summer. Behind the trees is the Foxton inclined plane, a late 19th-century engineering feat that lifted loaded barges up the hillside in a cradle. Today it is being renovated.

▼ **Foxton, The Grand Union Canal c1960** F159004
An empty barge, probably belonging to the British Waterways Board, is tied up in this summer view of Foxton Basin. Landscaping and advertising have increased the number of visitors to the locks and the adjoining charming village.

► **Gaddesby, The Church c1955**
G218002
St Luke's is a fine church in an equally well-proportioned village. Inside is a life-size monument to a Colonel Cheyney, sculpted in alabaster in 1848, showing him on one of the four horses shot from under him at Waterloo. The church is believed to have been founded by the Knights Templar from Rothley.

▲ **Hinckley, Market Place c1965** H266003
Two mothers with contrasting baby transport pass the market place. Still a going concern, Hinckley's busy market draws people from a wide area of Leicestershire and Warwickshire. The buildings on the left here have disappeared, whilst Simpkin & James, the District Bank and Nurseryland all have different occupiers. The parish church of St Mary is as unchanging as ever.

◀ **Glenfield, The Square and the Church c1960** G197010
Growth has seen Leicester all but engulf this large commuter village on the city's north-west outskirts. The small Co-op has given way to a superstore nearby. The village also has the world's first railway tunnel which is just over a mile long. The Leicester to Swannington line's first train was driven by George Stephenson. The railway brought coal prices tumbling in the town and ensured prosperity, along with other villages along the line.

Hinckley, Castle Street c1965 H266010 This selection of British cars is eye-catching. As in many other towns and cities, red brick is the dominant building material; it is used extensively for all types of buildings.

Hinckley, The Borough c1965 H266016
This broad street, with ample space for parking, displays contrasting architectural styles: the small 19th-century shops face mid 20th-century designs.

Hinckley, Station Road c1965 H266005
Easily recognisable today, this thoroughfare is still at Hinckley's heart. The ornate Billiard Hall, advertising full size tables, along with Parsons Sherwin and Co's buildings, have disappeared.

Ibstock, Main Street c1965 I48009
The town's growth came from the nearby coal mines - they are now closed. The most noted industry now is the well-known Ibstock brick company, which sells to customers world-wide. Restalls, on the right, extended in 1977 and took over Randalls next door. Similarly, the Ram Inn Hotel (the white building further down the street) also enlarged to include its neighbour.

▼ **Kegworth, The Post Office c1965** K139039

The now busy A6, along with the rapid growth of the nearby East Midlands Airport, compounds the traffic problems that Kegworth has seen since the M1 junction was put in a mile away. Here, though, in more tranquil days, St Andrew's, one of the largest of the county's churches, overlooks the village centre.

▼ **Kibworth Beauchamp, Church Road c1965** K119013

We are looking from beside the church of St Wilfred; the view is little altered today. However, the small village shop extension has disappeared. The Harborough bus is about to set off for Kibworth Harcourt, the neighbouring village, and two fine old family cars stand in the road.

▲ **Kibworth Beauchamp, Station Street c1955**

K119017

The station (left) was built on the site of the old rectory; it closed in 1968, and is now used as offices. The fine set of old cottages on the left were probably owned by the railway. They face the Railway Arms across the well-laid-out street. Note the caravan on the left beyond the 'torch of learning' school road sign.

◀ **Kibworth Harcourt, Leicester Road c1955**

K171015

The Rose and Crown Hotel, now on the main A6, stood on the old Leicester-Harborough-Northampton stage of the journey from the north to London, and at one time serviced twenty-four coaches; the horses were changed here, and the passengers were refreshed.

▼ **Kilby, The Dog and Gun c1960** K125012
Flanked by two extensions, the oldest part of this inn dates from the 17th century, and is an important building in today's village. It still has a rural atmosphere.

▼ **Kirby Muxloe, Main Street c1965** K126009
Enterprise House, on the left, almost doubled Kirby's shops when it opened. Today a new Royal Oak has replaced the one we see here. Kirby was the most blitzed English village during the last war: a lone bomber came over following a raid on the Midlands and destroyed many buildings.

▲ **Kirby Muxloe, The Castle c1965** K126007
There are no encroaching buildings and road systems yet in this view of the fortified Manor House, started in 1480 by Lord Hastings. It was never completed - Hastings was executed in 1483.

◀ **Langham, The Old Cottage and the Chapel c1960** L337011
The village's mid-Victorian Baptist chapel stands close to the 13th-century church of St Peter and St Paul. Picture postcard thatched cottages built of local stone mix pleasantly with Georgian and Victorian villas in this well-kept village. The original home of Ruddles Brewery, and a regular meeting-place of the Cottesmore Hunt, it remains delightful and interesting.

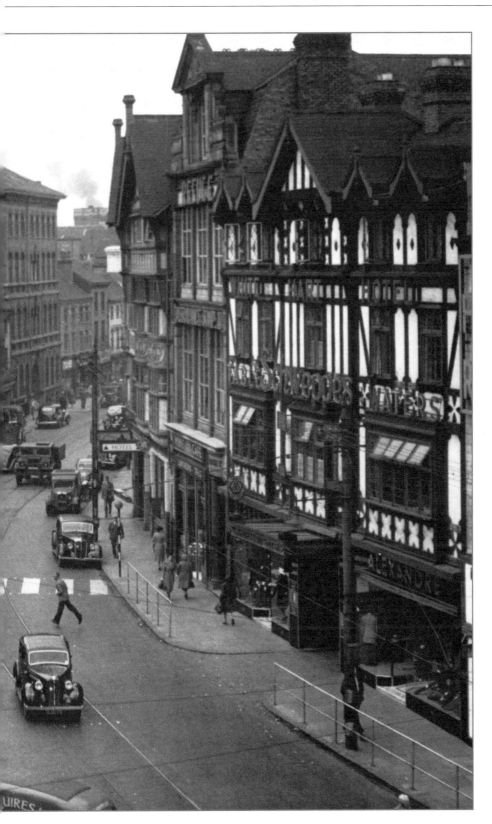

Leicester, The Clock Tower and Belgrave Gate c1950 L144006
Tram wires and tracks are evident in this view of the county town. With five important roads making this junction, it proved to be one of the most complicated tramway configurations in the world. The 1960s saw all but a few buildings on the left swept away. Note the fine White Hart Hotel and the adjoining buildings.

**Leicester,
Humberstone Gate
c1948** L144008
A selection of buses
and the odd tram
occupy one of the four
gates that surround the
clock tower. The two
buses parked on the
left are outside the Bell
Hotel, birthplace of the
Leicester-Swannington
railway, the first in the
Midlands. One tramline
disappears by the side
of the hotel through a
narrow gap to the
depot behind. All have
now gone, including
the large Lewis's
department store built
in classic 1930s style.

Leicester, The Clock Tower, City Centre c1955 L144056
This photograph shows Churchgate and Belgrave Gate viewed from Gallowtree Gate - 'gate' is derived from the Scandinavian, meaning 'a road to'. The illuminated Bovril sign was an integral part of the city centre scene for well over a decade.

Leicester, The Auto Magic Car Park, Lee Circle c1963 L144087
Almost brand new at the time this photograph was taken, the first multi-storey car park of this size in the country opened on the site of Lee Street, the birthplace of Joseph Merrick, the tragic Elephant Man. Note one of the city's first supermarkets - it is easy to park and shop in one place.

Leicester, De Montfort Hall c1955 L144126
De Montfort Hall has been used for nearly a century for all types of meetings, entertainment, education and civic celebrations. A host of stars have performed here, for the acoustics are first-class. Note the organ, one of the country's finest.

▼ **Leicester, The Town Hall c1965** L144024
Dating from 1875 with later extensions, the building replaced the old Guildhall which had served for municipal affairs since 1586. Its square was laid out in 1879.

▼ **Loughborough, Baxter Gate c1950** L197007
Buildings from the last two hundred years adjoin each other in a rather odd and uneasy way in Leicestershire's second town. The added floors of the General Hospital stand head and shoulders above the scene, which includes a mixed assortment of vehicles.

▲ **Loughborough, Market Place c1955** L197019
The middle section of well-remembered shops has now been replaced with department stores. The essence of a modern commercial centre is evident. Parking is at a premium, and it's not even market day!

◄ **Loughborough, Swan Street c1955** L197025
The Saracen's Head, tiled in the local Swithland slate, dominates this scene; it is little changed today.

Loughborough, Market Street c1949

L197028

This busy thoroughfare with a wide variety of shops was always well frequented. Today, while the right-hand side is almost intact, the left-hand side has seen major redevelopment to provide an even greater selection of businesses.

▼ **Loughborough, Queens Park, the Entrance c1953** L197040
This pleasant and colourful place lies in the town's centre. The tower contains a grand carillon of forty-seven bells. Built to remember the fallen of the Great War, it is a fitting tribute, for one of Britain's two bell foundries is in the town.

▼ **Loughborough, Wards End c1955** L197038
Offilers' Ales have long disappeared from the re-named Wheatsheaf. This view towards the market shows the wide variety of small independent traders that still flourish in the town.

▲ **Lutterworth, High Street c1955** L307003
The main road falls away to cross the River Swift and goes on to Rugby. The two towns are the places where the jet-age began: Sir Frank Whittle was designing and testing in the area from 1937.

◄ **Lutterworth, Church Street c1955** L307004
The commercial centre of the town for over a hundred years, this area had long-established tradesmen's shops. Lutterworth was not joined to a main railway until 1899; but the Great Central Line promoted tourism by displaying the town on its official postcards.

▼ **Market Bosworth, Market Place c1955** M233012
Time stands still on a summer's afternoon, with houses going back
four hundred years placed all around the square. The market is still
held here, and buyers and sellers come in from miles around.

▼ **Market Bosworth, Ye Old Red Lion c1955** M233007
At the time of this photograph, Hoskins, a family brewery in Beaumanor Road,
Belgrave, in Leicester, owned this, their one public house. Tom Hoskins, a
Worcestershire man, founded the concern at the turn of the century and
produced the selection that won him the highest awards for a variety of beers.
The adjoining ancient cottages have gone, and have been replaced with housing
that remains in keeping with the town.

▲ **Market Harborough,
Northampton Road
c1955** M33019
The coach road leaves
the town centre over the
River Welland, from
where this view was
taken. Many Georgian
houses throughout the
town remain, and its
buildings are always
worth a second look.

◄ **Market Harborough, The Ritz, Northampton Road c1955** M33020
Television was still in its infancy when 'Prince of Thieves' was entertaining local people here at The Ritz. The cinema finally closed its doors, only to be re-opened in its new role as a supermarket.

▼ Market Harborough, The Old Grammar School c1960 M33035

Wooden arches on stone pillars support the timbered walls and gables of this little gem. Note the ornamental barge boards. The school was founded in 1613 by Robert Smythe, a local man who made good in London. It is complimented by the parish church of St Dionysius next door.

▼ Measham, The Parish Church c1965 M234002

In the heart of the old coalfield, this large village had many inhabitants dependent upon the mine and its good coal. The church of St Laurence dates from the 14th century; its tower was rebuilt in the 1730s.

▲ Melton Mowbray, Cheapside c1955

M60076

In the background is St Mary's, said to be the most beautiful parish church in England. In a variety of tall and ungainly buildings, an assortment of traders await their customers; of those we can see, a third are chemists!

◄ **Melton Mowbray, Market Place c1955** M60107
The van belonging to Alfred Mason, Provision Merchant and Importer, makes a drop-off on its journey from Leicester in this busy view. Although all the buildings have changed trades, variety is as evident today as it was then.

**Melton Mowbray,
Market Place c1955**
M60078
Judging by the parked
cars, it is not a market
day. The upper
windows of Warner's
Café are attractively
surrounded with half-
crown tiles. Both
Warner's and Bailey's
across the square were
well-frequented on
market days.

◀ **Melton Mowbray, Nottingham Street c1965** M60114
At the time of this photograph, traffic was not excluded from this street. A delivery van stands beside the Olde Pork Pie Shoppe of Dickinson and Morris. The Melton area is world-famous for its pork pies, Stilton cheese and hunt cake. Next door to the Olde Pork Pie Shoppe is the Corn Exchange, later to have a new identity as the Bell shopping centre.

◄ Melton Mowbray, Market Place c1965
M60132
Ten years later, only Warner's appears to have changed hands. Pedestrianisation still seems a long way off.

▼ Melton Mowbray, Sherrard Street c1965 M60137
1930s and 1960s styles clash openly with the traditional buildings on the left. The Black Swan of Home Ales Brewery, a popular edge-of-centre inn, is facing the brand-new supermarket selling best salmon at 3s 11d a tin and its own-brand tea at 1s 3d per packet. Note the four unchained bicycles.

◄ Newbold Verdon, Main Street c1965
N144008
This large village with houses showing mixed building styles centres on the crossroads near St James's Church. Note the air raid siren above the door of the Old Black Swan.

Newtown Linford, The Village c1965 N96001
The village is the gateway to Bradgate Park, a very large medieval deer park, which was donated to the people of Leicester for recreation in 1928. Neatly-kept stone and timber-framed cottages punctuate the lane that is the main street. This area is described as a walkers' paradise; one of the many footpaths is signposted behind the school sign.

Newtown Linford, Bradgate Park c1965 N96012
In the heart of the park stand the ruins of Bradgate House, a Tudor mansion; it was the childhood home of Lady Jane Grey, the tragic nine-day Queen of England who was executed in 1553.

Oakham, Market Place c1955 O2022
Controlled growth has kept this, the largest town in England's smallest county, a pleasant and compact community. Its quaint and gracious market-place hosts some Royal Mail and GPO vans, plus a selection of post-war cars. Best ale in oak barrels is being delivered to the George Hotel, with some barrels blocking the pavement.

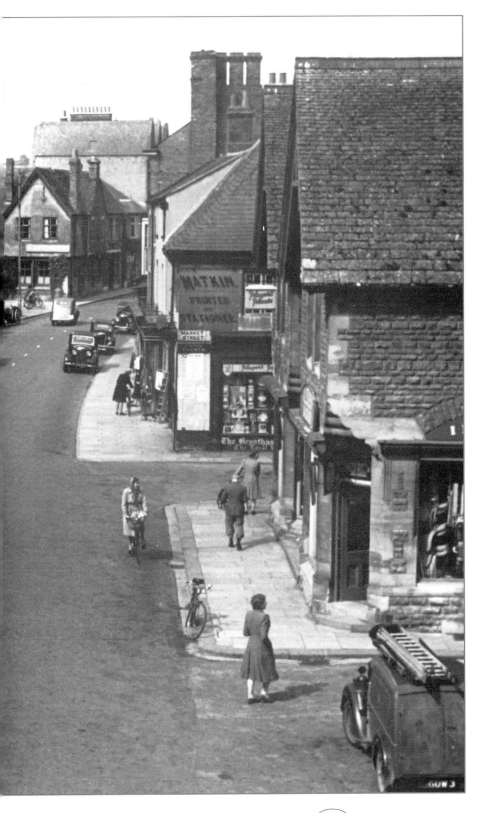

Oakham, High Street c1955 O2028
Still on view here is the home of Jeffrey Hudson, the world's smallest man, who hopped out of a pie to amaze Queen Henrietta, wife of King Charles II. A classic English market, surrounded by a variety of shops, meets on Wednesdays and Saturdays, drawing visitors and traders from far afield.

▼ **Oakham Castle, The Queen's Horseshoe c1965** O2063
This Norman hall has only recently stopped being used as a magistrates' court.
Here the visitor can find a remarkable collection of horseshoes in all sizes, for the
tradition of the town requires all nobility, including members of the Royal Family,
to present a horseshoe when visiting Oakham. The sovereign's gift is placed
immediately above the magistrate's chair.

▼ **Queniborough, The Village c1955** Q12002
Two inns, the Britannia (left) and the Horse and Groom, still occupy the centre of
this extended but fine country village that retains its atmosphere. The magnificent
oak tree has gone, unfortunately. In the last century the landlord of the Britannia
kept a pet bear, which regularly escaped to wander round the village!

▲ **Quorn, High Street
c1955** Q11010
The famous hunt often
meets at the crossroads
in the distance. The main
A6 is quiet as it passes
the White Swan. During
the last war, the
American forces
stationed outside the
village lived in Tent City,
and an avenue of lime
trees has been planted as
a memorial to them.

◄ **Rothley, Old Cottages Fowke Street c1955**

R259011

The village has been occupied since Roman times. It has been described as being fragmented, but here, in the centre, cottages of differing styles combine to give an air of rustic beauty. The position of the windows right under the eaves is typical of humbler houses.

◄ **Sapcote, The Post Office c1965** S485008
Later housing faces Victorian buildings on the edge of this large village. In days gone by, Sapcote was a centre for cheese-making and the framework knitting industry. Sapcote granite was also in constant demand for road-making and kerb stones.

Rothley, Fowke Street c1965 R259017
There has been some upgrading and renovation in the centre of this friendly village. Rothley has connections with the Knights Templar. Note the date 1727 between the ground and upper floor of the cottage on the right.

Seaton, The Viaduct c1955
S547001
Here we see the railway junction for the Uppingham branch, although little remains today to show that the railway passed through. In the distance is the former main line from London to Nottingham; it passes over the Welland Valley on the massive Harrington Viaduct, an engineering triumph of the 1880s.

Shepshed, The Bullring c1960 S497184
Shepshed used to be heavily involved in hosiery and knitwear, and the town still has links with its original industries. The Westminster Bank, a grandiose building in brick and buff terracotta, dates from 1903. Note the fully-laden coal lorry (centre).

Shepshed, Field Street c1960 S497186
The decorative brick house on the right is worth a second look. Groups of children, probably from St Wilfred's school at the bottom, occupy the street. This is a village of artisan housing and shops, dating mainly from the 19th century.

◄ **Sileby, Cossington Road c1965** S498007
The Free Trade Inn has served many generations in this industrial village. In the heart of the Soar Valley, Sileby is still home to workshops for various trades, hosiery and light engineering being the most important.

Sileby, High Street c1965 S498009
Here we see a fairly busy scene in the centre of this large and expanding village. Late Victorian shops exemplify the continuity of trading here; they shoulder up to earlier businesses, one of which has some timber framing (centre).

Smeeton Westerby, Main Street c1955 S742009
The winding main street of this conservation village passes many cottages built for those who worked the land. The cottages with their gable end built next to the street are generally far older than the rest. Halfway down on the left, an ironstone wall retains two mullioned windows from a former cottage. Because it was thought to add character to the village, it was saved from demolition.

South Luffenham, The Church c1955 S486004
A special memorial in the church of St Mary the Virgin is dedicated to Ruth Boswell, daughter of the King of the Gypsies. She died whilst the gypsies were encamped nearby, and was originally refused burial as she was not a Christian. This decision, however, was overruled by the local curate.

▼ **South Wigston, Countesthorpe Road c1960** S548004
These red brick terraces were built to house the employees of
hosiery and shoe manufacturers at the turn of the century.

▼ **South Wigston, Gloucester Crescent c1965** S548015
The mid 20th century saw the housing boom: around the towns and
cities, large and small estates were built on agricultural land. Here, the
very spacious and pleasantly laid-out corner of just such an estate
indicates the post-war planning and housing ideals. Note the bubble
car for inner-city shopping.

▲ **Swithland, The Village
c1955** S550001
The local slate-producing
quarry nearby provided
roofing and graveyard
tombstones for a large
surrounding area. Begun
in medieval times, the
slate industry finished in
the early 1900s. In this
view, almost unchanged
today, we can see the
essence of a typical
Charnwood village.
Pretty cottages with iron
latticed windows
compliment thatches old
and new all along the
main street.

◄ **Syston, The Clock Tower c1965** S488036
Apart from the Baker's Arms on Barkby Road corner and an extended bank, the village's main shopping area is now but a memory. The Regency and Victorian buildings along the Melton Road have been removed for redevelopment. The memorial to the fallen has found a new home in Central Park, as it was considered a cause of traffic congestion in this position.

◀ **Syston, St Peter's Street c1955** S488006
By the turn of the century the village was growing very quickly, although it was still far from urban sprawl. Victorian and Edwardian villas of red brick with bay windows were uniformly built for artisans in this area.

Syston, The Green c1955 S488022
The remarkable thatched newsagent and general store on the left is festooned with now collectable enamel signs. An isolated lamp in the centre doubles as a bus stop, whilst the brick buildings behind look a little incongruous between the old cottages that neighbour them.

Thurmaston, The Bypass c1965 T235011
In this photograph the bypass is deserted compared with today, and there are no traffic lights. The road alleviated a bottle-neck in the nearby village, allowing traffic an easier route to Nottingham, Newark, Melton and the east coast.

Tilton-on-the-Hill, The Village c1955 T236003
At 700ft above sea-level, Tilton-on-the-Hill is one of the highest villages in High Leicestershire. Commanding beautiful views in all directions, the village is situated where two ancient Bronze Age tracks cross. The foundations of the village inn are said to be Saxon.

Twycross, The Village c1960 T237002
Known for its world-famous zoo, the village has been carefully allowed to grow. On the Green, the memorial is in company with a smaller one to commemorate trees planted for the Coronation in June 1953. Its church of St James the Great contains the oldest stained glass in England, which is originally French - it was made in Paris in around 1145.

Uppingham, High Street c1965 U10071
We are looking towards the centre of this pleasant market town. A mixture of architectural styles makes an attractive picture; the early 18th century Crown Hotel is probably the best building in this street. Note the wide pavements, and the market stalls at the far end.

Uppingham, Market Place c1965 U10082
The late 18th-century post office on the left, with the Victorian
Falcon Hotel straight ahead, contribute to a charming square;
here, then as now, personal service and choice were important.
Friday markets have been held here for over seven hundred years.

Uppingham, Market Place c1955 U10032
The compact square has convenient tea-rooms in the left-hand corner. The square is overlooked by the church of St Peter and St Paul, which commands views of the town on one side and rolling countryside on the other. The post office completes the scene.

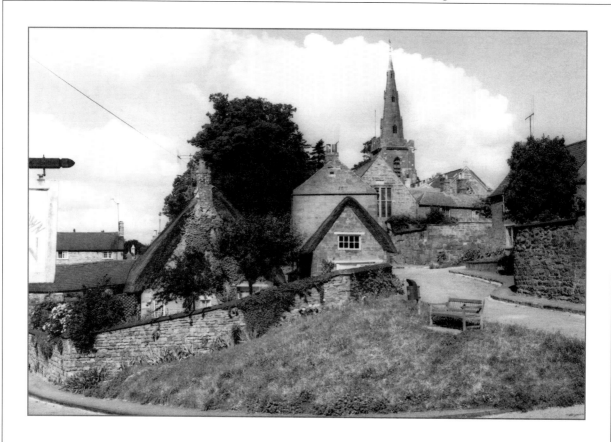

Uppingham, The Church c1965 U10075
This view of the church, which was taken away from the town
centre, also shows a pretty ironstone thatched house and
numerous houses roofed with the local slates. In the streets off the
market, many picture postcard gardens add to the attractiveness
of the town.

Whitwick, The Crossroads c1965 W365043
Whitwick is a mining village, and is set amid some of the best scenery of Charnwood Forest. As early as 1293 it was granted a weekly market and a four-day fair. This view shows Market Street.

Wigston, Leicester Road c1965 W366041
Before traffic calming started, the central shopping area of this large suburb had already seen some changes: note the 1960s building encroaching and replacing the Victorian terraces - some of them have been boarded up.

Witherley, The Church c1960 W531001
The River Anker flows slowly by St Peter's, which has served the village since 1173. From this placid view, only the middle cottage survives today. The village also houses the Atherstone Hunt stables and kennels.

Woodhouse Eaves, Main Street c1955 W367019
Set in the heart of Charnwood Forest, this pretty village was a favourite destination for Edwardian trippers, and features on many postcards. The essence of the village still holds firm, with some delightful cottages. Note the Swithland slate roof, small upper rooms and window shutters in this photograph.

Index

BIBLIOGRAPHY

W G Hoskins: *Leicestershire - A Shell Guide*

Leicestershire WI: *Leicestershire and Rutland Within Living Memory*

N Pevsner: *Buildings of England Series - Leicestershire and Rutland*

Arthur Mee: *The King's England - Leicestershire and Rutland*

Tourist Information: *Rutland Visitors' Guide*

Frith Book Co Titles

www.francisfrith.co.uk

The Frith Book Company publishes over 100 new titles each year. A selection of those currently available are listed below. For latest catalogue please contact Frith Book Co.

Town Books 96 pages, approx 100 photos. County and Themed Books 128 pages, approx 150 photos (unless specified). All titles hardback laminated case and jacket except those indicated pb (paperback)

Amersham, Chesham & Rickmansworth (pb)	1-85937-340-2	£9.99
Ancient Monuments & Stone Circles	1-85937-143-4	£17.99
Aylesbury (pb)	1-85937-227-9	£9.99
Bakewell	1-85937-113-2	£12.99
Barnstaple (pb)	1-85937-300-3	£9.99
Bath (pb)	1-85937419-0	£9.99
Bedford (pb)	1-85937-205-8	£9.99
Berkshire (pb)	1-85937-191-4	£9.99
Berkshire Churches	1-85937-170-1	£17.99
Blackpool (pb)	1-85937-382-8	£9.99
Bognor Regis (pb)	1-85937-431-x	£9.99
Bournemouth	1-85937-067-5	£12.99
Bradford (pb)	1-85937-204-x	£9.99
Brighton & Hove(pb)	1-85937-192-2	£8.99
Bristol (pb)	1-85937-264-3	£9.99
British Life A Century Ago (pb)	1-85937-213-9	£9.99
Buckinghamshire (pb)	1-85937-200-7	£9.99
Camberley (pb)	1-85937-222-8	£9.99
Cambridge (pb)	1-85937-422-0	£9.99
Cambridgeshire (pb)	1-85937-420-4	£9.99
Canals & Waterways (pb)	1-85937-291-0	£9.99
Canterbury Cathedral (pb)	1-85937-179-5	£9.99
Cardiff (pb)	1-85937-093-4	£9.99
Carmarthenshire	1-85937-216-3	£14.99
Chelmsford (pb)	1-85937-310-0	£9.99
Cheltenham (pb)	1-85937-095-0	£9.99
Cheshire (pb)	1-85937-271-6	£9.99
Chester	1-85937-090-x	£12.99
Chesterfield	1-85937-378-x	£9.99
Chichester (pb)	1-85937-228-7	£9.99
Colchester (pb)	1-85937-188-4	£8.99
Cornish Coast	1-85937-163-9	£14.99
Cornwall (pb)	1-85937-229-5	£9.99
Cornwall Living Memories	1-85937-248-1	£14.99
Cotswolds (pb)	1-85937-230-9	£9.99
Cotswolds Living Memories	1-85937-255-4	£14.99
County Durham	1-85937-123-x	£14.99
Croydon Living Memories	1-85937-162-0	£9.99
Cumbria	1-85937-101-9	£14.99
Dartmoor	1-85937-145-0	£14.99
Derby (pb)	1-85937-367-4	£9.99
Derbyshire (pb)	1-85937-196-5	£9.99
Devon (pb)	1-85937-297-x	£9.99
Dorset (pb)	1-85937-269-4	£9.99
Dorset Churches	1-85937-172-8	£17.99
Dorset Coast (pb)	1-85937-299-6	£9.99
Dorset Living Memories	1-85937-210-4	£14.99
Down the Severn	1-85937-118-3	£14.99
Down the Thames (pb)	1-85937-278-3	£9.99
Down the Trent	1-85937-311-9	£14.99
Dublin (pb)	1-85937-231-7	£9.99
East Anglia (pb)	1-85937-265-1	£9.99
East London	1-85937-080-2	£14.99
East Sussex	1-85937-130-2	£14.99
Eastbourne	1-85937-061-6	£12.99
Edinburgh (pb)	1-85937-193-0	£8.99
England in the 1880s	1-85937-331-3	£17.99
English Castles (pb)	1-85937-434-4	£9.99
English Country Houses	1-85937-161-2	£17.99
Essex (pb)	1-85937-270-8	£9.99
Exeter	1-85937-126-4	£12.99
Exmoor	1-85937-132-9	£14.99
Falmouth	1-85937-066-7	£12.99
Folkestone (pb)	1-85937-124-8	£9.99
Glasgow (pb)	1-85937-190-6	£9.99
Gloucestershire	1-85937-102-7	£14.99
Great Yarmouth (pb)	1-85937-426-3	£9.99
Greater Manchester (pb)	1-85937-266-x	£9.99
Guildford (pb)	1-85937-410-7	£9.99
Hampshire (pb)	1-85937-279-1	£9.99
Hampshire Churches (pb)	1-85937-207-4	£9.99
Harrogate	1-85937-423-9	£9.99
Hastings & Bexhill (pb)	1-85937-131-0	£9.99
Heart of Lancashire (pb)	1-85937-197-3	£9.99
Helston (pb)	1-85937-214-7	£9.99
Hereford (pb)	1-85937-175-2	£9.99
Herefordshire	1-85937-174-4	£14.99
Hertfordshire (pb)	1-85937-247-3	£9.99
Horsham (pb)	1-85937-432-8	£9.99
Humberside	1-85937-215-5	£14.99
Hythe, Romney Marsh & Ashford	1-85937-256-2	£9.99

Available from your local bookshop or from the publisher

Frith Book Co Titles (continued)

Ipswich (pb)	1-85937-424-7	£9.99	St Ives (pb)	1-85937415-8	£9.99
Ireland (pb)	1-85937-181-7	£9.99	Scotland (pb)	1-85937-182-5	£9.99
Isle of Man (pb)	1-85937-268-6	£9.99	Scottish Castles (pb)	1-85937-323-2	£9.99
Isles of Scilly	1-85937-136-1	£14.99	Sevenoaks & Tunbridge	1-85937-057-8	£12.99
Isle of Wight (pb)	1-85937-429-8	£9.99	Sheffield, South Yorks (pb)	1-85937-267-8	£9.99
Isle of Wight Living Memories	1-85937-304-6	£14.99	Shrewsbury (pb)	1-85937-325-9	£9.99
Kent (pb)	1-85937-189-2	£9.99	Shropshire (pb)	1-85937-326-7	£9.99
Kent Living Memories	1-85937-125-6	£14.99	Somerset	1-85937-153-1	£14.99
Lake District (pb)	1-85937-275-9	£9.99	South Devon Coast	1-85937-107-8	£14.99
Lancaster, Morecambe & Heysham (pb)	1-85937-233-3	£9.99	South Devon Living Memories	1-85937-168-x	£14.99
Leeds (pb)	1-85937-202-3	£9.99	South Hams	1-85937-220-1	£14.99
Leicester	1-85937-073-x	£12.99	Southampton (pb)	1-85937-427-1	£9.99
Leicestershire (pb)	1-85937-185-x	£9.99	Southport (pb)	1-85937-425-5	£9.99
Lincolnshire (pb)	1-85937-433-6	£9.99	Staffordshire	1-85937-047-0	£12.99
Liverpool & Merseyside (pb)	1-85937-234-1	£9.99	Stratford upon Avon	1-85937-098-5	£12.99
London (pb)	1-85937-183-3	£9.99	Suffolk (pb)	1-85937-221-x	£9.99
Ludlow (pb)	1-85937-176-0	£9.99	Suffolk Coast	1-85937-259-7	£14.99
Luton (pb)	1-85937-235-x	£9.99	Surrey (pb)	1-85937-240-6	£9.99
Maidstone	1-85937-056-x	£14.99	Sussex (pb)	1-85937-184-1	£9.99
Manchester (pb)	1-85937-198-1	£9.99	Swansea (pb)	1-85937-167-1	£9.99
Middlesex	1-85937-158-2	£14.99	Tees Valley & Cleveland	1-85937-211-2	£14.99
New Forest	1-85937-128-0	£14.99	Thanet (pb)	1-85937-116-7	£9.99
Newark (pb)	1-85937-366-6	£9.99	Tiverton (pb)	1-85937-178-7	£9.99
Newport, Wales (pb)	1-85937-258-9	£9.99	Torbay	1-85937-063-2	£12.99
Newquay (pb)	1-85937-421-2	£9.99	Truro	1-85937-147-7	£12.99
Norfolk (pb)	1-85937-195-7	£9.99	Victorian and Edwardian Cornwall	1-85937-252-x	£14.99
Norfolk Living Memories	1-85937-217-1	£14.99	Victorian & Edwardian Devon	1-85937-253-8	£14.99
Northamptonshire	1-85937-150-7	£14.99	Victorian & Edwardian Kent	1-85937-149-3	£14.99
Northumberland Tyne & Wear (pb)	1-85937-281-3	£9.99	Vic & Ed Maritime Album	1-85937-144-2	£17.99
North Devon Coast	1-85937-146-9	£14.99	Victorian and Edwardian Sussex	1-85937-157-4	£14.99
North Devon Living Memories	1-85937-261-9	£14.99	Victorian & Edwardian Yorkshire	1-85937-154-x	£14.99
North London	1-85937-206-6	£14.99	Victorian Seaside	1-85937-159-0	£17.99
North Wales (pb)	1-85937-298-8	£9.99	Villages of Devon (pb)	1-85937-293-7	£9.99
North Yorkshire (pb)	1-85937-236-8	£9.99	Villages of Kent (pb)	1-85937-294-5	£9.99
Norwich (pb)	1-85937-194-9	£8.99	Villages of Sussex (pb)	1-85937-295-3	£9.99
Nottingham (pb)	1-85937-324-0	£9.99	Warwickshire (pb)	1-85937-203-1	£9.99
Nottinghamshire (pb)	1-85937-187-6	£9.99	Welsh Castles (pb)	1-85937-322-4	£9.99
Oxford (pb)	1-85937-411-5	£9.99	West Midlands (pb)	1-85937-289-9	£9.99
Oxfordshire (pb)	1-85937-430-1	£9.99	West Sussex	1-85937-148-5	£14.99
Peak District (pb)	1-85937-280-5	£9.99	West Yorkshire (pb)	1-85937-201-5	£9.99
Penzance	1-85937-069-1	£12.99	Weymouth (pb)	1-85937-209-0	£9.99
Peterborough (pb)	1-85937-219-8	£9.99	Wiltshire (pb)	1-85937-277-5	£9.99
Piers	1-85937-237-6	£17.99	Wiltshire Churches (pb)	1-85937-171-x	£9.99
Plymouth	1-85937-119-1	£12.99	Wiltshire Living Memories	1-85937-245-7	£14.99
Poole & Sandbanks (pb)	1-85937-251-1	£9.99	Winchester (pb)	1-85937-428-x	£9.99
Preston (pb)	1-85937-212-0	£9.99	Windmills & Watermills	1-85937-242-2	£17.99
Reading (pb)	1-85937-238-4	£9.99	Worcester (pb)	1-85937-165-5	£9.99
Romford (pb)	1-85937-319-4	£9.99	Worcestershire	1-85937-152-3	£14.99
Salisbury (pb)	1-85937-239-2	£9.99	York (pb)	1-85937-199-x	£9.99
Scarborough (pb)	1-85937-379-8	£9.99	Yorkshire (pb)	1-85937-186-8	£9.99
St Albans (pb)	1-85937-341-0	£9.99	Yorkshire Living Memories	1-85937-166-3	£14.99

See Frith books on the internet www.francisfrith.co.uk

FRITH PRODUCTS & SERVICES

Francis Frith would doubtless be pleased to know that the pioneering publishing venture he started in 1860 still continues today. A hundred and forty years later, The Francis Frith Collection continues in the same innovative tradition and is now one of the foremost publishers of vintage photographs in the world. Some of the current activities include:

Interior Decoration

Today Frith's photographs can be seen framed and as giant wall murals in thousands of pubs, restaurants, hotels, banks, retail stores and other public buildings throughout the country. In every case they enhance the unique local atmosphere of the places they depict and provide reminders of gentler days in an increasingly busy and frenetic world.

Product Promotions

Frith products are used by many major companies to promote the sales of their own products or to reinforce their own history and heritage. Frith promotions have been used by Hovis bread, Courage beers, Scots Porage Oats, Colman's mustard, Cadbury's foods, Mellow Birds coffee, Dunhill pipe tobacco, Guinness, and Bulmer's Cider.

Genealogy and Family History

As the interest in family history and roots grows world-wide, more and more people are turning to Frith's photographs of Great Britain for images of the towns, villages and streets where their ancestors lived; and, of course, photographs of the churches and chapels where their ancestors were christened, married and buried are an essential part of every genealogy tree and family album.

Frith Products

All Frith photographs are available Framed or just as Mounted Prints and Posters (size 23 x 16 inches). These may be ordered from the address below. From time to time other products - Address Books, Calendars, Table Mats, etc - are available.

The Internet

Already twenty thousand Frith photographs can be viewed and purchased on the internet through the Frith websites and a myriad of partner sites.

For more detailed information on Frith companies and products, look at these sites:

www.francisfrith.co.uk
www.francisfrith.com
(for North American visitors)

See the complete list of Frith Books at:

www.francisfrith.co.uk

This web site is regularly updated with the latest list of publications from the Frith Book Company. If you wish to buy books relating to another part of the country that your local bookshop does not stock, you may purchase on-line.

For further information, trade, or author enquiries please contact us at the address below:
The Francis Frith Collection, Frith's Barn, Teffont, Salisbury, Wiltshire, England SP3 5QP.
Tel: +44 (0)1722 716 376 Fax: +44 (0)1722 716 881   Email: sales@francisfrith.co.uk

---

See Frith books on the internet www.francisfrith.co.uk

TO RECEIVE YOUR FREE MOUNTED PRINT

Mounted Print
Overall size 14 x 11 inches

Cut out this Voucher and return it with your remittance for £1.95 to cover postage and handling, to UK addresses. For overseas addresses please include £4.00 post and handling. Choose any photograph included in this book. Your SEPIA print will be A4 in size, and mounted in a cream mount with burgundy rule line, overall size 14 x 11 inches.

Order additional Mounted Prints at HALF PRICE (only £7.49 each*)

If there are further pictures you would like to order, possibly as gifts for friends and family, purchase them at half price (no additional postage and handling required).

Have your Mounted Prints framed*

For an additional £14.95 per print you can have your chosen Mounted Print framed in an elegant polished wood and gilt moulding, overall size 16 x 13 inches (no additional postage and handling required).

---

* IMPORTANT!
These special prices are only available if ordered using the original voucher on this page (no copies permitted) and at the same time as your free Mounted Print, for delivery to the same address

---

Frith Collectors' Guild

From time to time we publish a magazine of news and stories about Frith photographs and further special offers of Frith products. If you would like 12 months FREE membership, please return this form.

Send completed forms to:
The Francis Frith Collection, Frith's Barn, Teffont, Salisbury, Wiltshire SP3 5QP

Voucher for **FREE** and Reduced Price Frith Prints

Picture no.	Page number	Qty	Mounted @ £7.49	Framed + £14.95	Total Cost
		1	**Free of charge***	£	£
			£7.49	£	£
			£7.49	£	£
			£7.49	£	£
			£7.49	£	£
			£7.49	£	£

Please allow 28 days for delivery	*** Post & handling**	**£1.95**
Book Title	**Total Order Cost**	**£**

Please do not photocopy this voucher. Only the original is valid, so please cut it out and return it to us.

I enclose a cheque / postal order for £ . . . .
made payable to 'The Francis Frith Collection'
OR please debit my Mastercard / Visa / Switch / Amex card
(credit cards please on all overseas orders)

Number . . . .

Issue No(Switch only) . . . . .Valid from (Amex/Switch) . . . .

Expires . . . . Signature . . . .

Name Mr/Mrs/Ms . . . .

Address . . . .

. . . .

. . . . Postcode . . . .

Daytime Tel No . . . .   Valid to 31/12/03

The Francis Frith Collectors' Guild

Please enrol me as a member for 12 months free of charge.

Name Mr/Mrs/Ms . . . .

Address . . . .

. . . .

. . . . Postcode . . . .

Would you like to find out more about Francis Frith?

We have recently recruited some entertaining speakers who are happy to visit local groups, clubs and societies to give an illustrated talk documenting Frith's travels and photographs. If you are a member of such a group and are interested in hosting a presentation, we would love to hear from you.

Our speakers bring with them a small selection of our local town and county books, together with sample prints. They are happy to take orders. A small proportion of the order value is donated to the group who have hosted the presentation. The talks are therefore an excellent way of fundraising for small groups and societies.

Can you help us with information about any of the Frith photographs in this book?

We are gradually compiling an historical record for each of the photographs in the Frith archive. It is always fascinating to find out the names of the people shown in the pictures, as well as insights into the shops, buildings and other features depicted.

If you recognize anyone in the photographs in this book, or if you have information not already included in the author's caption, do let us know. We would love to hear from you, and will try to publish it in future books or articles.

Our production team

Frith books are produced by a small dedicated team at offices in the converted Grade II listed 18th-century barn at Teffont near Salisbury, illustrated above. Most have worked with the Frith Collection for many years. All have in common one quality: they have a passion for the Frith Collection. The team is constantly expanding, but currently includes:

Jason Buck, John Buck, Douglas Burns, Heather Crisp, Lucy Elcock, Isobel Hall, Rob Hames, Hazel Heaton, Peter Horne, James Kinnear, Tina Leary, Hannah Marsh, Eliza Sackett, Terence Sackett, Sandra Sanger, Lewis Taylor, Shelley Tolcher, Helen Vimpany, Clive Wathen and Jenny Wathen.